Ayurvedic Financial Freedom: Insights From My Wealth Journey

Diego Tresinari, Ph.D.
Center for Financial/Ayurvedic Studies,
Scientific Researcher (Engineering Economics/ Food Science and Technology)
Campinas-SP, Brazil
E-mail: diego_tresinari@yahoo.com.br
WhatsApp: +55.19.99805.0484

Keywords: Economics; Ayurveda; Financial Independence; Personal Finance; Investments; Self-knowledge; Money

Short Biography

Diego T.resinari holds a PhD in Food Science and Technology Field from University of Campinas (UNICAMP) (2011), Brazil. From 2011-2019 he worked as a scientific researcher in Food Engineering Department at the UNICAMP. Between 05/2013-04/2014 and 01/2016-12/2016 he did postdoctoral internships in Engineering Economics topic at the Swiss Federal Institute of Technology Lausanne (Switzerland) with Professor François Maréchal and at University of Valladolid (Spain) with Professor Dr. María Jose Cocero. Besides he did short-term visiting research period at Dublin City University (Ireland), at University of Chile (Chile) and at CONICET-Bahía Blanca (Argentine). He has published 85 papers in peer-reviewed journals, 8 book, 41 book chapters and more than 125 works in scientific conferences. Moreover, he developed 13 new scientific Processes/Products. He has participated in several research projects (45) with both, public and private funding. He has supervised 2 PhD theses, 6 MSc dissertations; 2 undergraduate and 8 visiting students' research projects. Among his many activities related to the promotion of scientific development, Dr. Diego Tresinari served as reviewer for 70 international journals and as member of the editorial advisory board for 12, in addition he also was part of the organizing committee of 7 scientific conferences.

Summary

Introduction	5
Financial freedom journey steps	9
Know yourself	16
Which biotype do you belong to?	24
Setting your strategy towards a financial freedom project	34
Freedom through money versus freedom from money	56
Insights from my financial freedom journey: Use compound interest in your favor	62
Insights from my financial freedom journey: Invest aiming financial freedom	72
Insights from my financial freedom journey: Define your life style	79
Insights from my financial freedom journey: Define a safe withdrawal rate	89
Anti-guidelines for performing an Ayurvedic financial freedom journey	95
Center for Financial Studies (Financial Consulting, Brazil)	99
Center for Ayurvedic Studies (Food Science and Ayurveda, Brazil)	100
Other Books: Liberdade Financeira Ayurvédica: Insights de Minha Jornada (Portuguese Edition)	101

Other Books: Ações com Lucidez: a Saga de um Investidor Iniciante na Bolsa de Valores (Portuguese Edition) 103

Other Books: – Investidor-Trader Lúcido: Acabando com a Polarização no Mundo dos Investimentos (Portuguese Edition) 104

BOOK SERIES (AMAZON) – Investimentos com Lucidez (Portuguese Edition) 106

INTRODUCTION

Dear reader, first, it is a pleasure that you decided to read this book. I have wondered about it for many years. To be more precise, since my girlfriend, currently my wife, and I started our financial freedom journey back in 2008. If you are not familiarized with this terminology, don't worry, because it will be further explained moreover. In a few words, financial freedom is the point when you do not have to work anymore, as the income that you receive from your investments is enough to pay all your monthly expenses.

Today my wife and I have a family with 3 children and we achieved the financial freedom point about one year ago. Therefore, my idea with this book is to present to you the insights that we had during our financial freedom journey.

In order to entertain you besides provide you some financial education, I will try my best talking about some parts of our life that can help you. During these approximately 10 years, we had been through several interesting situations that I am sure that you would like to know. We are a 34 years old couple from Brazil and we have visited more than 20 countries over these years, spending 4 short periods between 2-3 months in each country and 1 year living in Europe.

Before starting telling our history in a chronological way I would like mention about the last facts that pushed me towards writing this book. I started writing this book in October 1st of 2017, and exactly one week earlier I was in a Workshop about Finances with the most international experts. It was my first conference about this topic, my wife and I are scientific researchers at a University in Brazil, with Ph.D. titles in Engineering and I am very used to go to boring scientific conferences. I mean boring because now I can compare both kinds of events. It was the first time that the National Achievers Congress (NAC) was in Brazil and Robert Kiyosaki, author of the 20-year-old best-selling book "Rich Dad Poor Dad", was joining the event. I had read this book in 2009, and it was the first book that presented me the idea of financial freedom, (specifically Robert calls as financial independency, but the idea is the same). This book really touched me, so I went to that conference very excited to see my financial idol. The conference was very good and I really recommend you, if you have the opportunity, to go to such event. But it was completely different from what I expected. Besides Robert Kiyosaki a lot of speakers were also present. Although they were many, a common presentation approach was used. They used neuro-linguistic programming techniques and for several times emphasized to the audience that in order to be rich, they had to think as a rich person and so on. They explained that you should change your mentality or mindset to direct your life to earn money.

Looking back to my financial freedom journey I have to admit that my way was not like that. My wife and I did not change our mentality. We actually always had the sensation that becoming rich would be inevitable. Sooner or later we would get rich, and it was inevitable even though if we had not met each other. On the other hand, I felt pity for most people that were assisting the event because I knew that in the next day, they would try to change their mentality without success.

After this compassion moment, I had a flash remembering of a documentary about the dietary supplement company Herbalife that I saw in the beginning of the same year. In that documentary, a lawyers group was contacting some Herbalife's sellers and explaining them that they were not successful selling the products because the system is organized in a way that several people must fail so only few people can succeed.

Hence, from that moment I was kind of pushed towards telling people that the way to achieve something, it can be money, a better job, to become a better parent, or so on, is not changing your mentality. The way is to know yourself, know your mind and accept it as it is. Do not try to change anything. Love yourself as you are. Please do not waste your time, energy and money in this type of violent approach and schemes organized to rob you. I have tried to change myself in some aspects of my life and failed, and it was very disappointing. I will get in more details next and also explain what worked for me and I have seen working for many. Thus, I invite you to discover how exciting and amazing can be your financial freedom journey accepting our way of been. Have fun.

Diego Tresinari

March 2020

Chapter 1

FINANCIAL FREEDOM JOURNEY STEPS

"The journey of a thousand miles begins with one step."

Lao Tzu

Well... Since I invited you to discover how exciting and amazing can be your financial freedom journey, I will firstly tell you about the main steps that you will go through. I like the idea that we find in financial freedom books and articles that describes the journey as a climbing of a mountain. With a similar approach, I will describe the financial freedom journey steps as a climbing of a stairs. I prefer the use the stairs representation since there is no end to a staircase. When you think that the stairs are not enough, you can build another floor and connect to the old stairs. If you are climbing a mountain you do not have the possibility of continuing climbing when you achieve its top. The financial freedom is achieved at the point where your investment income is enough to pay all your monthly expenses. But if you want to increase the expenses due to any reason, for example, you would like to move to another city with higher life cost, or you had a baby, or any other reason, you will probably have to build another step at your staircase and go further.

This is happening with my wife and me right now. As I mentioned before, some months ago we achieved this freedom point and instead of being very happy, start thinking about quitting our jobs and living at the beach to always be light clothed, barefoot and drinking "caipirinha" or coconuts water (given that I am from Brazil) we started thinking about the next step of the stairs.

Maybe, this can be a surprise for you. But I have seen the same behaviour from different people that achieved the financial freedom point. I felt surprised myself when, at the beginning of our financial freedom journey, I heard about those free people that kept living the same life.

Indeed, I thought they were mad, workaholic or things like that, to keep working without need. But today I understand them. Of course, my wife and I felt an ecstatic relieve when we did the math and realized that we could quit our jobs. Probably, the same emotions some athletes fell when they win an Olympic game. But, as the Olympic winners, just a few weeks after achieving their goal, there is a rush to start the preparation for the next competition, even knowing that the next competition is not as important as the last one was.

What can be behind this phenomenon observed with several people like me? Given that I am a scientific researcher, I am very used trying to find literature and/or propose an explanation for my findings. Here, using the latter approach, I can suggest that the problem is related to the energy that you have mobilized to achieve the ending point. This energy is so great that it cannot be dissipated so easily. To corroborate with that, you can observe that this behaviour does not occurs to people that got rich playing the lottery. Lottery winners can easily do nothing after receiving the prize money. Actually, some of them were already doing nothing before getting rich. I am not saying that in a pejorative way, I am just indicating that some people are very practical and work well and some are not. In the next chapter, I will present some facts about different types of personalities and how you can use your personal attributes to get rich. Even if you are a kind of a lazy worker, I will show you strategies of how to be successfully financial free your own way.

As I have already talked about the last steps of the journey, let's start talking about the first ones.

See below a scheme (Figure 1) of the financial freedom journey steps.

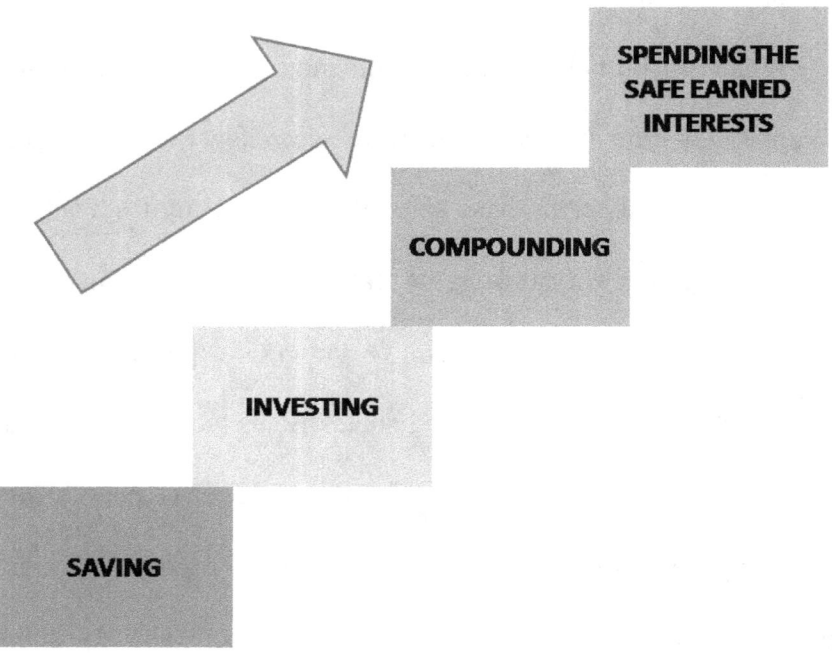

Figure 1. A scheme of the financial freedom journey steps.

Saving step: This is the first step. In this step you start saving the difference of your income and expenses. So, obviously, if you cannot save any money, game over, just when the game was in the beginning.

Investing step: In this second step you should start increasing your financial education in order to learn how to invest your saved money, like reading this book for example. Please do not ask for any financial advisor that works for a financial company where it is better to invest your money. They will probably sell you the best product for his interest and not yours, as they normally receive commission for each financial product sold. Actually, I do not recommend you to ask anyone, because in my opinion the best option would you know yourself and find the best way that works for you. But, if you really want to ask someone then, you should try to find an independent financial advisor, someone that does not receive commission for selling financial products. They should charge you only for the time that they spent understanding your financial situation and for the explanations and suggestions.

Compounding step: With continuous compounding, any interest earned immediately begins earning interest on itself, thus this is the way of helping your money work for you. In the next chapters, I will give several examples about this fantastic compounding phenomenon.

Spending the safe earned interest Step: Finally, the final step is when you can quit your job and start living from the interests. Since I am currently going through this step and could not find good literature about this topic, I will do a special effort to write a specific chapter on this subject.

Just for curiosity I have searched in the internet how many millionaires there are in Brazil today and found out that there are only 160.000 people, which is only 0.16 % of the current working population. Maybe at your country, this percentage can be a little bit different but probably relatively low too. The calculation is done considering only individuals older than 18 years that have more than 1.000.000 Brazilian Reais (R$) [Approximately 340.000 American dollars (US$)][1] in assets (investments that gives you money), excluding the value of the house that you live. Nevertheless, we cannot say that all the calculated millionaires are financial free, as it is dependent on the ratio of expenses per income. Therefore, if their expense is much higher than their income, they still will have to work. Thus it is

---

[1]In 2018 1 US$ was around 3 R$

worth discussing about this last step carefully. But first let's talk about the most important issue of this book in my opinion: self-knowledge.

Chapter 2

KNOW YOURSELF

"To know thyself is the beginning of wisdom."

Socrates

Probably you have already listed about the importance of self-knowledge from several people. For sure, they argued that knowing oneself is important in many aspects of your life and it can also have a positive impact on your financial path. But, I am not certain if you have found someone that could help you with the self-knowledge process. It is really a process and I am only in the beginning of it, but fortunately I have been in touch with a tool that helped me a lot to start this process and maybe can help you too.

I am really tired of people saying that to become rich you should think as a rich person, that all the rich people have some patterns so you have to copy these behaviours and the problem is solved, and so on. Before finding the tool that I will introduce you, I have studied coaching and Neuro-Linguistic Programming (NLP) and I have tried my best to use several techniques indicated by these "Financial Gurus". More precisely, I did not applied theses techniques to get richer financially, but to stop drinking alcohol. I was addicted to alcohol since I was a teenager. My addiction was not the common alcoholic addiction, that of someone that drinks every day, disturbing their whole life. My addiction, on the other hand, was of someone that only gets drunk during the weekends, in parties or while going out with friends. This is very common in Brazil nowadays and I could note the same behaviour among young people while living in Spain. However, this teenager addiction did not stop when I became a young adult, neither when I became a father. So I struggled hard trying to find a solution.

After trying psychotherapy I realized a few things. First, every person that I knew that was going through therapy or had being in to therapy simply took many years to understand the problem roots and many didn't deal with the problem. In therapy many people try to find the "responsible" person by its default. A mother that worked too much, a father that was never there, the fact that the person is an only child of a marriage; anything could be the target to a risk behaviour like mine. But what is the solution? I realized that to find a cause or to be more precise to rationalize about my addiction problem or any other problem in order to create a theory about its roots would not help me in the moment that I would be facing a beer, for example. I also realized that my therapist was also on therapy, and probably his therapist could be in therapy, and that this fact is actually very common and acceptable. That stroked me very weirdly that time, being treated for someone that was in treatment himself. I felt that probably both of us didn't have a clue to what we were doing. So I started looking for other methods and tools and found coaching and NLP.

The principles behind both techniques, coaching and NLP, are very good. They are focused on the fact that we as human beings are more robot like as we thing. We have several old patterns and habits that are very linked with our nature. On the other hand, discover the common behaviours of the rich people and imitate them is not for sure the way to success. And if you do that, the only thing that you will attain is to be a really robot like person, as you will be an unauthentic person. But the choice is yours.

Thus, what could really help me? Which was the way to problem solving? The way for me was very natural, after several years I realized that I was applying a common oriental psychology-based method without being conscious of that. In the beginning, I reduced the amount of beers that I was drinking. Before starting drinking, I usually planed how many cups or bottles I would drink and restricted the drinking to that limited amount. I also changed the environment that I used to drink. I didn't drink any more at parties. I kind of became a beer's taster, only drinking beer at quiet places with a friend. And slowly my hungry to get drunk reduced a lot. Then I felt ready to do the last step and reduced the amount of beers to zero. So, in that moment, I felt in control of my addiction and not drinking made no difference to me, I didn't need to.

After overcoming my addiction by accidentally becoming a conscious beer taster, I started reading a book about oriental psychology, i.e. psychology developed in the eastern countries, such as India, China, Tibet, Japan, etc. At that very moment, I couldn't stop falling in love with it. Based on that knowledge, I could understand that when I became a beer's taster I was applying a method called mindfulness or attention awareness. It was only by chance, following my instincts, that I changed the unconscious heavy drinking habit to a more conscious or mindful habit of tasting artisanal beers with a friend in a very calm place. If you have studied and/or experienced coaching and NLP, you could say that the same result could be achieved with help of an expert in these techniques and I agree with you. But the point is that, I would be dependent of an expert for overcoming problems, exactly as the therapist needs therapy. And also, these techniques can solve the problem, but I would not be aware of the real solution that is becoming conscious of each moment. The heavy drinking problem was probably linked to a "forever young wish" to get back to teenager years, a therapist would have probably diagnosed me as suffering from "Peter Pan syndrome" (you know the history, right? About a kid that never wants to grow up). I could say that the drinking problem was the scenario but it was not the real goal of the method that worked for me, as being conscious was a solution that could be applied to every problem in my life.

So let's do the link between increasing your consciousness and how to improve your financial situation. Maybe you are not saving money because you have the habit of spending all the money that you have.

Maybe you are not saving money because you never thought about it and you are just unconsciously moving with the ordinary people, buying the last cell phone, the latest car and house, etc. Thus, let's have a break and start thinking about if all your expenses are being done with awareness.

If your answer is "no, I am not complete aware of my financial expenses and choices" then I have an exercise for you. From now on, you will have to start doing a mindfulness technique during several periods of your day. For example, when you wake up you can do a brief exercise of breathing in front of the mirror in order to be aware that you are up and breathing. I do this exercise together with singing a very short yoga mantra, if you practice yoga you can choose one that you know and do it like me. If you do not practice yoga you can do only breathing observation, the effect will be the same. During the day if you have any free time as you are waiting a friend to arrive or you are at the bus stop, instead of doing ordinary things that will only keep you unconscious and away of the present moment you can do the same breathing observation for 5-10 min too. Finally, during the night you can do like me, and do breathing observation meanwhile you wash the dishes in a very attentive way.

I do not know if you have already done any meditation practice. If not, in my opinion, this way of dish washing is the best way to start, since you can see very easily when your mind start wondering around and forgetting about the dish washing and the process becomes mechanic. Since you have done it several times, you start thinking about other things, like have I paid that bill? Which day is today? What should I do after finishing this? Etc. Thus, after 1-2 months of mindful doing the dishes you can infer from your own experience that your mind works in a way without asking you any permission. In other words, you can realize that what your mind wants is not necessarily what you conscious want. And finally, you can conclude that you are not your mind, that you are the observer that is watching your mind working. In the beginning, it can sound a little bit mystic since maybe you are not familiar with it. But I really ask you to not stop reading this book right now. In the following parts, with other examples, I think that it can be better understood.

Thus, since you did not thrown away this book, it is time to do the same mindfulness dish washing exercise but now at any moment that you make money related decisions. I did it once when I was shopping to find a gift to a friend, and the experience was very great. I could note my thoughts ranging from "I should buy it" to "I shouldn't" and from "I am sure that she will like this gift" to "I do not care about her reaction". Another exercise that could be very interesting is to be conscious while watching television marketing. Focus on how your mind reacts with it, probably your mind will response affirmatively to some products or maybe you will fell a tremendous will to buy something that you would never buy and that you don't really need. After observing your mind, you probably will feel the need to change things in your life. In my case, I threw away the television and started only watching streaming channels online and also paid YouTube to not see any more advertisements.

During my studies about oriental psychology and ancient wisdom, I came across a knowledge that could be helpful to set us in an economical freedom path as it kind of predicts what reaction your mind will have in determined situation. I also spent some time analyzing and talking to people around me to validate and understand this mind predicted reactions according to this knowledge. In next chapter this technique is presented in more detail.

Chapter 3

WHICH BIOTYPE DO YOU BELONG TO?

"Ayurveda is generally understood as 'Science of life' translating 'Ayur' as life and 'Veda' as science."

Ayurveda is an ancient system which, like yoga, has only one purpose: to expose the illusions of the mind. Before achieving this latter goal, Ayurveda has the first goal of bringing the body back into balance so it can heal itself. Since this book is not related to improving your body health, I will not get in details about this part. On the other hand, the Ayurvedic teachings are also related to the human psychology. This part is not very used for its practitioners, but in my opinion, it can be extremely helpful for someone that wants to develop financial freedom skills like you.

From my point of view, Ayurveda teachings are based on behaviour observations. I say that because I am a pragmatic person. If you search for the Ayurveda history, you will find a kind of religious explanation for its beginning. Thus, for us what is very important is that today we can observe similar patterns from people that we know as those described in the Ayurveda books dated from at least 5.000 years ago.

I discovered Ayurveda around 4 to 5 years ago, but as child I lived in a small and very traditional village which got me in contact with several ancient proverbs. Also, more recently, while living in Spain, I was in contact with several elder people and their knowledge. I know that some ancient proverbs are only bullshit, and some were only created to dominate you, but you can agree with me that some are very true. Trying to find which proverb is true or false is not the purpose. But, I would like to start with the assumption that, in most of the cases, your old grandmother would probably select someone for a new job more properly that you, even if you work in human resources and has a Bachelor's Degree in Psychology. An explanation for that may be that she has more years of life experience and observations than us. Unconsciously, she has observed during her life the small differences between human beings and which ones will make them suitable for each job/activity, or to be a good friend or not, and so on.

Other group that is very intelligent in biotype identification is the children. If a child does something wrong he will prefer to talk to someone that is friendlier with him, more frequently to his mother, instead of telling to someone that is harsher like a conventional father.

Therefore, here I will explain to you the 3 biotypes that Ayurveda describes: Vata, Pitta and Kapha in order to help you to realize in which group you probably belong aiming at helping you to plan your financial freedom journey.

Vata Biotype

A person that is considered a Vata biotype is commonly very creative and prefers activities that he/she can develop it widely. If you work in a closed office doing paper work and are not felling well probably you are a Vata biotype. Maybe you already have observed that you have this Vata nature and you have selected a job that you can move easily, as do jobs that require travelling, or that doesn't have a fixed routine.

Here I do not describe any profession that is good or bad for any Ayuvedic biotype since it depends a lot. Maybe you are a Vata-type person working as a secretary in an office and are not felling bored since you are in contact with people from different countries, fulfilling your Vata nature having new conversations with interesting foreign people every day.

Regarding finances, a person that has a strong Vata nature normally spends his/her money also in a very creative and not controlled way. I have a very close friend that spends a lot of money with his travels. He likes to visit exotic places, which is normally very expensive during holidays.

My recommendation to him is to always try to visit these places during common dates and also to do a financial plan before each travel. Another recommendation that I give him is to find a job that requires travelling. In that way, he can travel for free and work during some days or months, which would be very exciting for a Vata biotype like him.

In summary, in the Ayurveda scriptures they say metaphorically that a person that has a more pronounced Vata nature has more amount of the natural element air in their mind so their thoughts are more related to movement.

Pitta Biotype

A person that is considered a Pitta biotype is commonly disciplined and prefers activities that he/she can develop it widely. The Ayurveda practitioners say that a person that has a more pronounced Pitta nature has more amount of the natural element fire in their mind so their thoughts are more intense and explosive.

If you always try to improve the way you do an activity and also you are aware of how the others are performing the same activity to compete with them, probably you are a Pitta biotype. Maybe you already have observed that you have this Pitta nature and maybe you are suppressing this nature or adding more fire to it in an unconscious way, like choosing to work in competitive jobs and to leisure in competitive hobbies.

Regarding money, depending on how the Pitta type sees money, he/she can be very successful in the financial freedom journey or not. He/she can compete with the neighbour who has the most expensive car and/or house, on the other hand, the Pitta type also can compete for the best salary and/or the higher amount of money at the saving account.

I have a more pronounced Pitta nature and I used it consciously to easy my economical freedom path. At the beginning, I used my disciplined nature to increase my salary as soon as I could. My first income was a master fellowship in 2008 with the value approximately of 1.000 Brazilian reais (R$). One year after that, I got a Ph.D fellowship and my salary was increased around 80 %, resulting in a value of R$ 1.800. In 2011, my salary achieved around R$ 5.000. Therefore, I multiplied my salary by 5 in a period of 3 years. But it achieved its maximum when I was granted with a fellowship to go to Switzerland in 2013, receiving a salary of around R$ 17.000 (Approximately 5.500 American dollars (US$)]. It was 17 times higher that my master fellowship I had 5 years earlier. It was not a question only of money, I wanted to be the best in my field from the beginning, since my master studies. Therefore, I worked hard and converted my master study in the first year of my Ph.D and finished it in 3 years also earning the Brazilian prize of the best thesis of the year 2011.

Maybe you have achieved or you know someone that achieved similar professional records and you are thinking that a Pitta type sooner or later will get stomach problems and/or a heart attack. And you are right, but, since this book is only related to money aspects I will not talk about health problems. Thus I will describe the last Ayurvedic nature that can help balance the Pitta nature towards wealth.

Diego Tresinari, Ph.D

Kapha Biotype

A person that is considered a Kapha biotype is commonly lovely and prefers activities that he/she can develop it widely. In Spain, I heard an ancient proverb that says that if you are a person too sweet (like a Kapha person) probably you will get diabetes.

If you like to watch romantic movies and you feel attached to everything that you have, probably you are a Kapha biotype. Maybe you already have observed that you have this Kapha nature and maybe you are trying to become more similar to the typical Pitta biotype, as a pressure to earn more money, and it is not working.

In my opinion, the extreme valorization of the Pitta biotype is the worst thing that our modern society is doing, besides environmental destruction and wars. So, if you are trying to become more rational like the Pitta-type in order to become rich, I recommend you to stop it and try another strategy. Also, having a high salary is not a guarantee that you will get rich.

My strategy to the Kapha-type person is to accept your nature. You can use this nature in your favour by attaching yourself to the correct thing, money for example. Before I said that Kapha nature can help balance the Pitta nature towards wealth. It is true. But, what is also true is that Pitta nature can help balance the Kapha nature towards wealth. Thus, in this book I propose that to be rich Pitta and Kapha natures have to be balanced in order to optimize simultaneously the two sides of the "getting rich equation" (Figure 2), i.e. increasing the income using Pitta nature towards developing a strategy to get a high salary and/or a high investments or royalties income and decreasing expenses using Kapha nature.

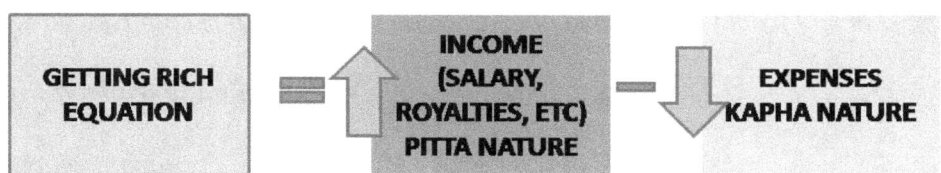

Figure 2. Getting rich equation.

Chapter 4

SETTING YOUR STRATEGY TOWARDS A FINANCIAL FREEDOM PROJECT

"The lion cannot protect himself from traps, and the fox cannot defend himself from wolves. One must therefore be a fox to recognize traps, and a lion to frighten wolves."

Niccolò Machiavelli

So let's start your financial freedom project. But before that, please read again the phrase from Machiavelli above. As I told you before, with the Ayurveda teachings we could predict your mind reaction to the above phrase. The first step is to be alert and conscious while reading such a profound phrase in order to react to it, which would be very difficult for a Vata-type person. A Kapha-type maybe be aware of the negative reputation of the terminology Machiavellian, which was denoted after Niccolò Machiavelli, probably by a Kapha-type person or society. The definition of Machiavellian in the dictionary is related to be cunning, amoral, strategist, which for a Kapha type are bad habits. Finally, if you are a Pitta-type you probably would like the quote and will use it as an aspiration in order to improve yourself to become a fox-lion being to frighten wolves and escape from the traps.

Therefore, based on your response to the reading of Machiavelli's sentence, we can set your strategy towards financial freedom project.

If you have identified a unique more pronounced nature in yourself, first you have to identify the intensity of it. In the previous chapter I explained in a very simple way the 3 natures with the example of someone having 100% of each nature in order to present you the extremes. I know a few people that are so unbalanced that you can say that he/she has almost 100% of only one of these 3 natures. On the other hand, most of the population has the 3 natures in a more balanced way.

For example, I have said that I have a more pronounced Pitta nature, but I know that I also have a significant amount of Vata nature too. It could be easily observed while reading the introduction text "We are a 34 years old couple from Brazil and we have visited more than 20 countries these years, spending 4 short periods between 2-3 months and 1 year living in Europe." My wife and I love to travel and find it too hard to stay a long time in a specific place.

If we could see the nature of a person being a XYZ graph, being X – Vata, Y – Pitta and Z – Kapha natures, and X+Y+Z = 100%. In my case for example I have around 50% Pitta, 40 % Vata and 10% Kapha (Figure 3). You may think: Only 10% Kapha? Yes, it is very difficult to me to have thoughts similar to a Kapha person. This is not bad or good, it only is, and this is the way my mind works. I am being completely sincere to you and therefore I ask you to be also very sincere to yourself and go through this self-knowledge process before setting your financial freedom strategy.

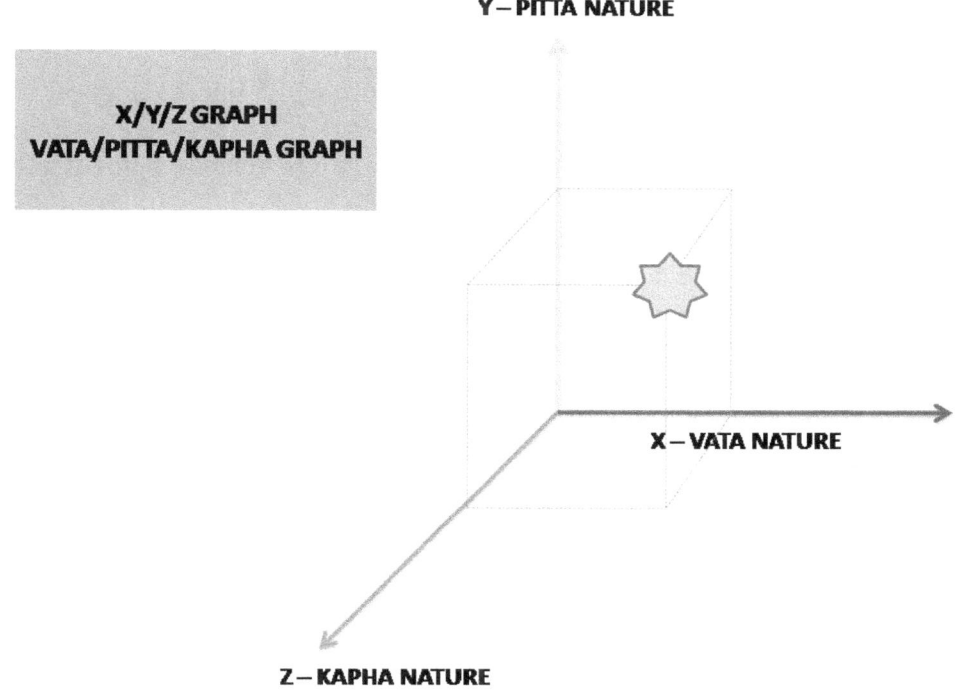

Figure 3. My X – Vata/Y – Pitta/Z – Kapha natures graph.

If you do not feel very confident about your Vata, Pitta and Kapha percentages right now, you have two options. One, you can continue reading the book with the first impression that you had about your nature and its percentages, and after adjust the strategy according to the improvement in your self-knowledge. Or, the other option would be to stop reading this book right now and only return to it after defining the

Vata, Pitta and Kapha percentages by observing first your close friends and family members during at least 2-3 months and then yourself. This exercise is very powerful and you will probably improve a lot your Ayurvedic biotype identification skill. I do it continually without effort and it is very helpful knowing the people that I am talking to, besides understanding the reason why each person is or isn't rich and successful. Recently I used this method to understand the author of a book that I was reading. This author had written a very confusing book but with several very creative ideas into it. So I assumed that probably he would be a Vata-type person, which was confirmed when I watched his interview talking about the book. The same observation could be applied to the way that I, as a writer. At the beginning of the book I said that because I worked as a scientific researcher I decided to write this book based on observations and numbers, but the real cause could be because of my Pitta nature. Pitta-nature people usually love number, methods, etc. The Chinese people commonly call the Pitta nature Yang (masculine energy) and the Kapha nature Yin (feminine energy). It is related to the general idea that man and woman are attracted to different things. Men are described to be more attracted to intellectual issues as number, method and strategies, and woman to be more nurturing and patient. If you are a woman and felt very insulted by my argument, it is not a generalization. Also, indignation is a very good reaction towards getting rich. You demonstrated right now that you have a high percentage of Pitta nature in you. So let's use it in your advantage while designing your financial freedom path. Thus please read the next section of this chapter.

Pitta-oriented strategy

For a better understanding, here I will start describing first some tips for a person with a more pronounced Pitta. Since my approach to getting rich in this book is based on my financial freedom journey, it is more didactical to start with the Pitta-oriented strategy related to the left part of the "getting rich equation".

If you are a Pitta type, i.e. has a higher percentage of Pitta nature, and you are not getting rich, it is probably because you are spending all your salary with expensive cars, houses, hotels, etc. After realizing it, you may feel the urge to revert this situation as soon as possible making up for the lost time looking for higher profitability at high risk investments. As I understand you since we have a similar mind, I should inform you that this is not the best way to start a financial freedom project. It is very dangerous to start investing in high risk investments without the correct mentality and knowledge. For instance, I found the stock market or maybe the stock market found me in the first steps of my journey. Obviously, my Pitta nature got very excited about the idea of getting extremely high valorization quickly. On the other hand, I consciously kept this market very far until 2014 (6 years after) and preferred to invest first at the real estate market and after in government bonds, etc.

As a first step, I recommend you to start increasing the Kapha part (right part) of the "getting rich equation", related to reduce your expenses in order to increase your savings.

How can I do it? I stopped talking about my wife in the previous chapters but now she is the key point. In our opinion she has around 35% of Kapha, 35% of Vata and 30% of Pitta natures, so we kind of used unconsciously her Kapha nature to reduce our life costs. And what is very interesting is that the first time that my grandmother met my wife, that time she was my girlfriend, she had: "My grandson is very lucky because he found a very Kapha girlfriend". She obviously did not use the word Kapha since we are from Brazil not from India, but the idea was the same. At that time I did not realized the profound wisdom of my grandmother, wondering that getting rich was more related to amount of salary earned than anything. I also thought that my grandmother had sympathy for my girlfriend because she is also very avaricious regarding money, which probably was also true.

Hence, for a Pitta-oriented strategy, since you probably have a good salary, you should start doing effort towards reducing life costs with the help of a Kapha-type person. It can be your own partner (wife or husband) that has a Kapha nature or a friend, a business partner, a family member or a financial consulting professional with high Kapha nature. It is really important to a Pitta type person to find someone with more pronounced Kapha nature in order to see how other person's mind works and to absorb naturally some of their behaviors, balancing your Pitta nature. Here I say naturally absorb not hardly change your mindset in a kind of hypnotic way.

Sometimes less is more. One tip to find a Kapha person is to use the half full-half empty glass quote. A more pronounced Pitta would be an optimistic person, always describing the glass half full, while a pronounced Kapha person would be pessimistic.

In the first years of my financial freedom journey, the use of the engineering economic performance indicator: 'Percentage of income saved' was the best choice that my wife and I did. This indicator can be very good for both Pitta and Kapha persons since it can be used in a competitive way, as the higher the number the better, and also as a conservative way indicating how much of the salary is being saved.

In 2009, after 1 year of starting our financial freedom journey, we got a mortgage to buy one Apartment near the University that we were working as Master students (If you have not defined the initial date of your journey do it right now. It can be a past date or a future date. This definition is very important in order to differ that you are not only saving money for the future, instead you are starting a project with beginning, performance indicators and end).

Today it sounds very crazy that only having a temporary salary (a two years Master fellowship) of R$ 1,200 each one (total income of R$ 2,400) we accepted pay a mortgage of R$ 2,400. Thus, we initiated saving 100% of our salary (R$ 2,400/R$ 2,400 X 100). In terms of 'Percentage of income saved' the day that we signed the contract with the owner of our Apartment, that we lived until last year (2019), we had the performance indicator of 100%. On the other hand, we planned in the following days to find someone to share the Apartment with us paying R$ 600 of rent. It reduced the value of 'Percentage of income saved' to 80% (R$ 2,400/R$ 3,000 X 100). And it worked very well, a couple from Colombia that we already knew and were looking for a place to stay, as they were like us doing Master at the same University, rented the other bedroom of the Apartment. Besides the money, we built a very good friendship with them. It resulted in a guided travel to Colombia and we stayed hosted in their family house.

Regarding the referred example, for a Pitta-type like me I honestly preferred thinking about it as I was doing leverage with the rent of our bedroom. In that way instead of having a 'Percentage of income saved' of 80%, my mind organized it, in order to push me towards the final score of financial freedom journey, as being a leverage of R$ 600, which was equivalent of half of my salary.

With these detailed examples about how my Pitta-oriented mind works, I thing that you can understand the idea and I hope that you can be able to watch your mind and use this information for a good purpose for you, regarding finances or not.

Kapha-oriented strategy

For a person with a more pronounced Kapha nature, obviously the strategy to be set for a successful financial freedom journey would be very different from a Pitta-type person. As I said before I have around 50% Pitta, 40 % Vata and 10% Kapha. With only around 10% Kapha, it is very difficult to me to have similar thoughts of a Kapha person. Therefore, my approach here will be based not in my own thoughts, but in my observations when having relationships with Kapha-type person, like my wife and my grandmother, for example.

The Kapha nature, in my opinion, is much more important than the pitta nature in the "getting rich equation", since the impact of reducing life costs is much higher than increasing salary and/or increasing interest rates or royalties incomes, for example. I will demonstrate it numerically to you next.

Imagine that your total monthly expenses are 4,000. I will not put any currency as it does not matter in this exercise. If you obtain 0.5% from your investments discounting inflation rate you need a total capital of 800,000 to be financial free. If your monthly expenses is only 12.5 %

higher, i.e 500, (500/4,000 X 100 = 12.5 %) you will need to save more 100,000 (200 X 500), which will indicated that you need to work for more several months. If you can save 500 you will need to work for more 200 months (more than 16 years). Considering a salary of 5,000, 500 would be a 'Percentage of income saved' of 10 %, which is the most common ratio adopted in Brazil for public employee pension plans. Obviously, you can save more, but the idea here is to demonstrate that to increase your life cost in only 500 (12.5 %) to pay your monthly expenses you will need to save 200 times the same amount. If you save the double percentage of your income, i.e. 20 %, the time will reduce to half, 100 months (more than 8 years), which is still a very long period. Instead of saving more you can increase your investment risk and get the same time reduction, but in my opinion it would be financially intelligent not increase the monthly expenses.

If you do the opposite, i.e. reduce in 500 your monthly expenses (total monthly expenses of 3,500), you will see the enormous advantages of using your Kapha nature towards financial freedom achievement. If your monthly expenses are reduced in 500 you can retire around 16 to 8 years earlier, since you will need a total capital of 700,000 instead of 800,000.

Maybe it is difficult to think about reducing your expenses right now. And I am not telling you to do it. I am only trying to provide you some insights that can help you to achieve the freedom of not needing to work anymore. Specifically, in my case, reducing my monthly expenses was not something that I would think first. But, motivated by getting my financial freedom some years earlier (2016), with the help of a person with a more pronounced Kapha than me, my wife, we reduced our monthly expenses in R$ 1,000, which represented 22.22% reduction, since our monthly expensed was R$ 4,500 and became R$ 3,500 (4,500-3,500/4,500 X 100 = 22.22 %). You can be wondering about which kind of money expenses we have reduced or that it is not worth to live a life within harsh restrictions. I can assure you that the expenses that we reduced were selected after thinking too much in order to avoid the felling of being trapped and that we had no freedom. It was a moment of study and deep analysis of our life and values what made us think about life and life choices in general. We got in touch with several life philosophies that helped us acquire the necessary strength to keep following our decisions. Among them, I can enumerate some: Ayurveda, Yoga, Buddhism, Minimalism, Environmentalism, Solidarity economy, etc.

The first budget cut that we made was in the cleaning service for our house. We had a cleaning lady once a week to help with the cleaning and tidying of our Apartment. We decided to dismiss her and to do this job ourselves. This step was not difficult since we lived in a small 2-bedrooms Apartment and the maid only helped us once a week, which was more symbolic than a real help since the other 6 days we took care of the cleaning. Actually, my wife kept saying to me that she thought that now the Apartment was more tide and clean because we felt responsible for its cleaning. If something was out of order or unclean, we had to take care of it right away and didn't wait for someone to do it in three days from now. My wife and I have a friend which her parents are from Japan. She was educated to think that having a maid was not proper since each one should be responsible for its own garbage and cleaning. In principle, this idea sounded a little bit rare to me. But when I saw that it could reduce in R$ 400 my monthly expenses, reducing consequently the time that I needed to achieve the financial freedom point, I completely changed my mind. Here I have to emphasize that I never repressed myself, I only got in touch with a new idea and kind of fell in love with it. If you repress yourself probably your decision will not be a long-term decision. I also didn't do any kind of neurolinguistic reprogramming, hypnosis or something like that. The approach was more based on understanding and valorizing the logic behind the Japanese mentality. Nowadays, besides having responsibility for my garbage and cleaning, I also extended that idea for my children's care. I do not contract babysitters, my wife and I are completely responsible for our children's care. And it was a great idea, as spending time with my kids is definitely the best Kapha part of my day. By the ways, I can realize that I have increased my Kapha percentage by this new activity.

The other reduction we chose to do was related to our health insurance plan. We decided to quit the private health insurance. In Brazil we all citizen have the free health insurance, so free access to doctors and medical treatment. But it doesn't work perfectly, there are big lines for routine medical appointments and hospitals are kid of full. So it is very common to medium and high class workers to have their own private health insurance. This latter reduction, which was a monthly reduction in R$ 600, was more difficult to be done since we had to reeducate our minds related to the fear of getting sick. It can sound a very radical decision and maybe it really was. It was a challenging situation, very attractive for a Pitta-type person like me, which motivated me to achieve with success the goal of not paying health insurance plan since then. In our life with health insurance, my wife and I had already some problems with the traditional health care system, and we started not agreeing with the way that the system was taking care of us. This became more pronounced when we had our first son in 2011 and the traditional health care system in Brazil tends to prefer caesarean instead of natural birth. So learn about Ayurveda (Ayurvedic Medicine) was more like a desperate search than an occasional meeting.

With these detailed example about how my wife Kapha-oriented mind worked, I thing that you can understand the idea and use this information for a good purpose for you, regarding finances or not. Here, I only emphasized one specific example about how a Kapha-oriented strategy can be applied to achieve financial freedom sooner since in this example my Pitta nature balanced my wife Kapha-oriented strategy. When we first started talking about reducing our expenses, my wife was not comfortable to reduce everything in order to achieve as soon as possible our financial freedom since she also has a prominent Vata nature, that fights for freedom. So I balanced her by convincing her to reduce only the few most significant expenses in terms of cost and the most insignificant ones in terms of personal pleasure and freedom. For example, we kept and still increased the amount of money we have saved for having coffee in an open air cafeteria (Vata-type person loves it). Even when we lived in Switzerland, we happily paid for each cappuccino 5 Swiss francs (the price of approximately 5 cappuccinos in Brazil) what made us happy after all.

The main problem of a more pronounced Kapha nature is that he/she doesn't know when to stop accumulating. Finding the balance should be the main point during a Kapha-oriented financial freedom strategy setting. Further I will give more ideas of how to stop your desire of having more money accumulated and never wanting to expend it. Unfortunately, my grandparents, which have both a high Kapha nature, are in this situation for years and do not enjoy expending their money that they worked so hard saving, thus I wouldn't like to see you going through the same.

Vata-oriented strategy

The most difficult task, in my opinion, is to set a getting rich strategy for a person with a more pronounced Vata nature, since they normally spend their money in a not controlled way. Unfortunately, the probabilistic of a Vata nature person getting rich is against them. You can notice that usually your friends that are artists, musicians, dancers, etc., i.e. Vata-type persons usually have money related problem. To apply the approach of investing the money that you save from your salary with Vata nature people is usually difficult since in addition they select jobs not thinking in money, which is not very good regarding financial freedom aspects. A solution would be either the Vata-type person balances his/her own nature or he/she should associate with a Pitta or Kapha-types person to help him/her to follow the long-term financial freedom path.

Choosing your work could be one way of balancing the Vata nature. A work that involves a sane amount of competitiveness could increase your Pitta nature and help you to set goals. A work that requires you to take care of people or animals could help you increase your Kapha and, therefore, take better care of your money as well, decreasing your expenses. If balancing your Vata nature is not possible or not enough to set you at the right money path then you will need to find a money partner to help you. To increase your probability of success you will have to be a specialist in reading your partner mind, as choosing to take the financial freedom journey with a Pitta or Kapha-types person. The chosen partner should be someone that you trust a lot, could be a husband/wife, a mother, a brother or other person that will be very sincere to you and will always be present. A Pitta-type partner could help you setting your saving goals and making you stick to it with perseverance. He could focus in the intelligent use of his competitive nature to increase your income by giving you ideas and alternatives to use your talent. A Kapha person could help you with understanding what is really important in your life and making a reduction cost plan but also being careful to make you comfortable with your saving goals so you do not fell blocked.

To choose careful your partner to getting rich is essential as you can find many Pitta or Kapha-types person with no inclination to the financial freedom path. For example, a Pitta-type person can compete with other people who spend more money. A Kapha-type person can accumulate things in his home without any commercial value such as books or things that only consume money from your pockets like cars (liabilities) instead of collecting properties for renting (assets). None of them will get to the freedom point where money is not a problem anymore, as money and usually a lot more money will be necessary.

Recently, a Vata-type friend of mine, an artist, asked me help because she was very concerned about her money situation. Talking to her I realized immediately the reason she was always running up so many debts. Also, the lack of money had nothing to do with the common sense that says that artists are not well paid. My suggestion to her was to create a very well paid business in which she would teach kids alternative dancing; a kind of flow dance. I had already seen her dancing with her child this flow dance and having a lot of fun. So the idea was pretty simple, she would book a time in her schedule, once or twice a week, to dance with her kid and also let it open to other kids to participate. She should charge what she felt was enough for a dance class. In the beginning she was very excited, but after only a few minutes all the enthusiasm was gone. As Ayurveda teachings say metaphorically, the movement of the Vata nature takes too much energy and quickly dissipates. While I was taking to her about the steps necessary to set this new dancing class I observed her energy dissipating in front of me. Thus, if you notice this nature within yourself, please do not be disappointed. After its acceptance, ask someone to help you to do the further steps that you cannot do alone. So you can keep your creativity and moving Vata energy dancing.

Chapter 5

FREEDOM THROUGH MONEY VERSUS FREEDOM FROM MONEY

"Reading minds skills, which comprehends to understand your own mind and of your partner's, can be a very powerful tool to help you to get rich."

Diego Tresinari

In the previous chapters I have emphasized a lot the advantages of watching your own mind before setting your strategy towards the financial freedom project. I finalized my argumentation with a very pessimistic opinion about the setting of a Vata-oriented strategy, i.e. strategy for a person which has a more pronounced Vata energy. In this chapter, I will talk about an exception that could happen.

Given that I have a secondary Vata nature constitution, I frequently had and still have Vata-type thoughts that could sabotage me during my financial freedom journey. On the other hand, another thought, which also is provided from the same Vata source, also appeared balancing the first one. This permanent thought was that I could attain freedom through money. Meanwhile, for the aim of getting rich, a Pitta-type person can be motivated by ambition, ambition to get money, power, prestige and so on; and a Kapha-type person can be motivated by fear, fear of lacking money or comfort, the comfort and safety that money can give. A Vata-type person can use as motivation the desire for freedom. And from my experience, money allied with self-knowledge really can bring you the aimed freedom that the Vata nature in yourself intrinsically wants.

On the contrary, if you have so little Vata nature in you, probably you will not fell that desire for freedom and will be trapped in the money saving cycle (Figure 4). You may think that being trapped in this cycle is much better than having any money or be trapped in the medium class cycle. But I can assure you that freedom from money should be your goal to have a fulfilled and happy life.

I know that I have a very difficult work to do. First, I have to motivate you to save money and then to do the right use of your intrinsic energy. If you have a Pitta nature, I have to help you to turn this energy towards the right target, i.e. financial freedom. Or, if you have a Kapha nature, I have to change your well trained mind so you don't get trapped in the saving money cycle. Yes, it can seem almost impossible, but I still think that you can enjoy a lot your journey as you do it, as I am doing with mine.

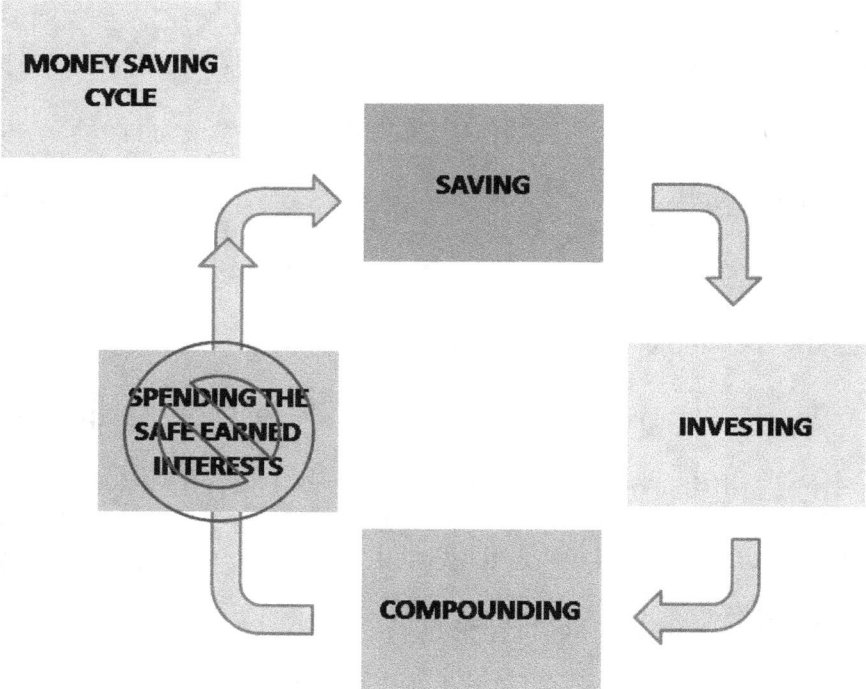

Figure 4. Money saving cycle.

Ayurvedic Financial Freedom: Insights From My Wealth Journey

When I was a teenager and had already lost that illusion that my father was a hero, I had a kind of insight of my father Ayurvedic nature. My father was a very slow driver, one could say he was a very careful driver, but without a doubt any passenger would get extremely bored in a 30 minutes drive and would ask him to please hurry up a little. In one of this never-ending trips, while I sat bored looking through the window, I started thinking about the correlation between the way people drive and their personality. It was clear to me that my father had very low "fire", in other words "Pita" nature, he was a very careful person, a "Kapha" type person. The funny story is that my mother was the opposite. She drove very fast, cursing people in her way and being very upset with slower trucks and cars at the middle of the road. It was no surprise that their marriage ended just a few years after I was born. They were so extremely different that they could not understand each other, neither in the daily life nor at their finances. While they were together they could not save any money. My mother had an extremely high salary that she spent it all and my father had a low salary, although he saved a little, he used much of it playing in lotteries trying to get rich. After they got divorced, my mother realized she was doing everything wrong about money, she had no savings, no house and Brazil was going through a very difficult economic time with big inflations. She had to start from zero, she had lost her job and the Apartment she had because of the economic situation, so she moved to a new city with me and got a new job. This time she was more careful, more because of the situation and the need than because of her nature, and with the passing of the years she could build a comfortable life. Now she is a retired lady, over 60 years old, but with enough money saved and with an easy life. My father history was a little different; it didn't have such a happy ending. When my parents got divorced, my mother stayed with the family Apartment that had a mortgage that she could not pay and lost it all. My father stayed with a saving account that had enough money to almost buy one Apartment, than it came the recession and the inflation went skyrocket. He was so attached to his money that he didn't want to touch it. He was very afraid of losing it. So he didn't move it to an investment that would protect its value, he didn't study and only relied in wrong bank financial advices. So within a few months the money that he had lost its value and he also had to star from zero. But his history didn't improve, he got remarried and although he always save money he doesn't know how to invest it, and he refuses my help, and always end up losing money value or stuck spending it in liabilities like cars.

This example shows how you can break the cycle or be kept in it without getting any freedom or peace, if I can say so. It also highlights the significance of knowing what to do with the money saved, what kind of investments and profitability one should aim while going through the financial freedom path. Some insights on this matter will be given in the next chapter.

Chapter 6

INSIGHTS FROM MY FINANCIAL FREEDOM JOURNEY: USE COMPOUND INTEREST IN YOUR FAVOR

"Compound interest is the eighth wonder of the world. He who understands it, earns it ... he who doesn't ... pays it."

Albert Einstein

The first insight from my financial freedom journey that I will share with you is related to the use of compound interest in your favour. With continuous compounding, any interest earned immediately begins earning interest on itself, thus this is a way of helping your money work for you. I started with this insight because compounding ability is always underestimated by the beginner investors.

After the achievement of my financial freedom point I started to teach, in the University that I worked as researcher, how to invest money to young people of 18-20 years old. The first question they had usually was related to how to maximize the investment rate of return. Every time I tried to convince them that it is better and safer to focus on maximize compound interest in your financial freedom journey.

I commonly use 3 examples in my classes, thinking that part of the students are probably more ambition (Pitta-type) than the another part (Kapha and Vata-types). The first example that I use is that the money can work for you. Like any good professional, it starts getting better as a worker within time and consequently it also gets higher remuneration as time advances. So it is better that you hire it as soon as possible in order to have a long time to see its improvement. The second example is for the people that dreams to work in a company, that covers health insurance and private pension, i.e. fear oriented Kapha-type persons. For them, I try to convince them that compounding works like a company that helps you to cost your personal private pension. In the beginning the company helps you with only a small percentage compared with your personal deposits, but around 10 years it is like the company is helping you with the same amount that you are depositing monthly and after only 15 years the company are paying 2/3 of the total monthly deposit and you only 1/3. Finally, for the Vata-type persons my argument is that compound interest is the best way to work less, get financial freedom and get retired travelling around the word.

Below (Figure 5/Table 1) I will present some numbers in order to demonstrate to you the real power of compounding that let Einstein shocked and makes me laugh every day that I look at my money growing up without my effort. And I only contracted my best employee 10 years ago, thus imagine the way it will be after 20-30-40-50 years from now.

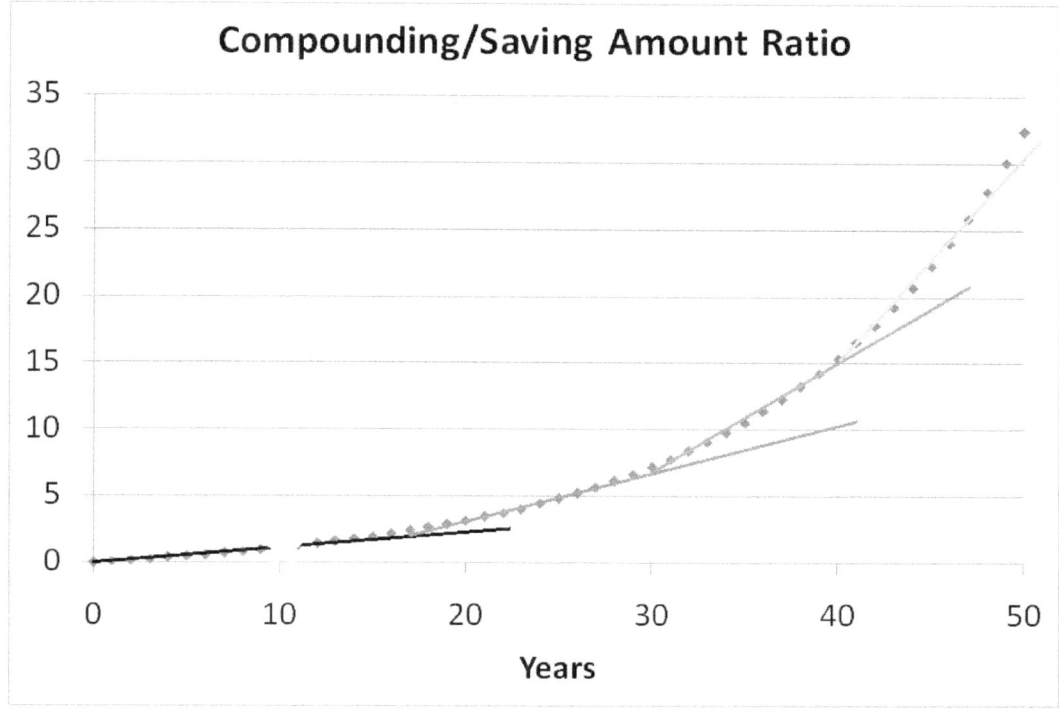

Figure 5. Compounding/saving amount ratio effect over time using simulated data.

Table 1. Equity and compounding/saving amount ratio evaluation effect over time using simulated data.

Year	Saving Amount (Monthly)	Saving Amount	Equity	Compound Interest Amount	Compound Interest/ Saving Amount Ratio
1	R$ 500.00	R$ 6,000.00	R$ 6,000.00	R$ 540.00	0.09
2	R$ 525.00	R$ 6,300.00	R$ 12,840.00	R$ 1,155.60	0.18
3	R$ 550.00	R$ 6,600.00	R$ 20,595.60	R$ 1,853.60	0.28
4	R$ 575.00	R$ 6,900.00	R$ 29,349.20	R$ 2,641.43	0.38
5	R$ 600.00	R$ 7,200.00	R$ 39,190.63	R$ 3,527.16	0.49
6	R$ 625.00	R$ 7,500.00	R$ 50,217.79	R$ 4,519.60	0.60
7	R$ 650.00	R$ 7,800.00	R$ 62,537.39	R$ 5,628.37	0.72
8	R$ 675.00	R$ 8,100.00	R$ 76,265.76	R$ 6,863.92	0.85
9	R$ 700.00	R$ 8,400.00	R$ 91,529.67	R$ 8,237.67	0.98
10	R$ 725.00	R$ 8,700.00	R$ 108,467.34	R$ 9,762.06	1.12
11	R$ 750.00	R$ 9,000.00	R$ 127,229.40	R$ 11,450.65	1.27
12	R$ 775.00	R$ 9,300.00	R$ 147,980.05	R$ 13,318.20	1.43
13	R$ 800.00	R$ 9,600.00	R$ 170,898.26	R$ 15,380.84	1.60
14	R$ 825.00	R$ 9,900.00	R$ 196,179.10	R$ 17,656.12	1.78
15	R$ 850.00	R$ 10,200.00	R$ 224,035.22	R$ 20,163.17	1.98

Ayurvedic Financial Freedom: Insights From My Wealth Journey

16	R$ 875.00	R$ 10,500.00	R$ 254,698.39	R$ 22,922.85	2.18
17	R$ 900.00	R$ 10,800.00	R$ 288,421.24	R$ 25,957.91	2.40
18	R$ 925.00	R$ 11,100.00	R$ 325,479.15	R$ 29,293.12	2.64
19	R$ 950.00	R$ 11,400.00	R$ 366,172.28	R$ 32,955.51	2.89
20	R$ 975.00	R$ 11,700.00	R$ 410,827.78	R$ 36,974.50	3.16
21	R$ 1,000.00	R$ 12,000.00	R$ 459,802.28	R$ 41,382.21	3.45
22	R$ 1,025.00	R$ 12,300.00	R$ 513,484.49	R$ 46,213.60	3.76
23	R$ 1,050.00	R$ 12,600.00	R$ 572,298.09	R$ 51,506.83	4.09
24	R$ 1,075.00	R$ 12,900.00	R$ 636,704.92	R$ 57,303.44	4.44
25	R$ 1,100.00	R$ 13,200.00	R$ 707,208.36	R$ 63,648.75	4.82
26	R$ 1,125.00	R$ 13,500.00	R$ 784,357.12	R$ 70,592.14	5.23
27	R$ 1,150.00	R$ 13,800.00	R$ 868,749.26	R$ 78,187.43	5.67
28	R$ 1,175.00	R$ 14,100.00	R$ 961,036.69	R$ 86,493.30	6.13
29	R$ 1,200.00	R$ 14,400.00	R$ 1,061,929.99	R$ 95,573.70	6.64
30	R$ 1,225.00	R$ 14,700.00	R$ 1,172,203.69	R$ 105,498.33	7.18
31	R$ 1,250.00	R$ 15,000.00	R$ 1,292,702.03	R$ 116,343.18	7.76
32	R$ 1,275.00	R$ 15,300.00	R$ 1,424,345.21	R$ 128,191.07	8.38
33	R$ 1,300.00	R$ 15,600.00	R$ 1,568,136.28	R$ 141,132.26	9.05
34	R$ 1,325.00	R$ 15,900.00	R$ 1,725,168.54	R$ 155,265.17	9.77
35	R$ 1,350.00	R$ 16,200.00	R$ 1,896,633.71	R$ 170,697.03	10.55
36	R$ 1,375.00	R$ 16,500.00	R$ 2,083,830.74	R$ 187,544.77	11.37
37	R$ 1,400.00	R$ 16,800.00	R$ 2,288,175.51	R$ 205,935.80	12.26

38	R$ 1,425.00	R$ 17,100.00	R$ 2,511,211.31	R$ 226,009.02	13.22
39	R$ 1,450.00	R$ 17,400.00	R$ 2,754,620.32	R$ 247,915.83	14.25
40	R$ 1,475.00	R$ 17,700.00	R$ 3,020,236.15	R$ 271,821.25	15.36
41	R$ 1,500.00	R$ 18,000.00	R$ 3,310,057.41	R$ 297,905.17	16.55
42	R$ 1,525.00	R$ 18,300.00	R$ 3,626,262.57	R$ 326,363.63	17.83
43	R$ 1,550.00	R$ 18,600.00	R$ 3,971,226.21	R$ 357,410.36	19.22
44	R$ 1,575.00	R$ 18,900.00	R$ 4,347,536.56	R$ 391,278.29	20.70
45	R$ 1,600.00	R$ 19,200.00	R$ 4,758,014.86	R$ 428,221.34	22.30
46	R$ 1,625.00	R$ 19,500.00	R$ 5,205,736.19	R$ 468,516.26	24.03
47	R$ 1,650.00	R$ 19,800.00	R$ 5,694,052.45	R$ 512,464.72	25.88
48	R$ 1,675.00	R$ 20,100.00	R$ 6,226,617.17	R$ 560,395.55	27.88
49	R$ 1,700.00	R$ 20,400.00	R$ 6,807,412.72	R$ 612,667.14	30.03
50	R$ 1,725.00	R$ 20,700.00	R$ 7,440,779.86	R$ 669,670.19	32.35

In the presented simulation it was considered an inflation rate of 5 % and an interest rate of 9 % per year, which is an approximation to the Brazilian rates at the time that this book was written (2017-2020). The saving amount considered, considering the inflation correction of it each year, was fixed at R$ 500.00 monthly (US$ 170.00[2]), total of R$ 6,000.00 (US$ 2,000.00) in the first year. This amount, in my opinion, is relatively

---

[2] In 2018 1 US$ was around 3 R$

affordable for most of the middle-class people from Brazil. For example, in 2009, in the beginning of our financial freedom journey, my wife and I saved monthly R$ 2,400.00.

The use of inflation was considered in order to keep the money value over time. Thus, in the second year, instead of only R$ 6,000.00 an amount of R$ 6,300.00 should be saved in order to eliminate inflation effects.

As said before, in Table 1, it was indicated that around 9 to10 years the same amount that it is deposited (R$ 8,300) is gained by the interest rate compounding, and after only 15 years the compound interest amount generated will be representing 2/3 of the total monthly deposit [R$ 20.163.17/(R$ 10,200.00 + R$ 20,163.17)]. Therefore, the amount earned with compounding interest that year (R$ 20,163.17) will be almost twice (1.98 times) of the amount saved R$ 10,200.00 in the same year. Meanwhile, in the year number 5 the opposite is observed, since R$ 3,527.16 is gained with interest rate compounding and R$ 7.200,00 is the amount saved from salary that year.

If you are not excited by the numbers I presented, I can show you a few more. For example, if you start with the financial freedom plan described of saving R$ 500.00 monthly this year, after 26 years the amount earned with compounding interest will be 5.23 times of the amount saved R$ 13,500.00 (calculated taking into consideration the value of R$ 6,000.00 saved in the first year of your plan). And, if you have enough patience to keep your plan for more 24 years, in the year 50 of your financial freedom plan the amount earned with compounding interest (R$ 669,670.19) will be 32.35 times of the amount saved from salary that year (R$ 20,700.00). So to start as soon as possible is the best way to initiate your financial freedom journey as financial mathematics is concerned. On the other hand, if you are not 20-30 years old and probably do not have 50 years to live from now, please do not become anxious.

Changing a little bit the perspective in order to inspire the most readers as possible to do your own financial freedom journey you can fix your vision in the amazing total amount of R$ 7,440,779.86 (approximately R$ 7.5 million = US$ 2.5 million) after 50 years, if you started at the age of 20 years old you would be an multimillionaire when arriving at 70. If you only want be a Brazilian millionaire a few less years is required, only 28-29 year, so following a plan like that saving R$ 500.00 (US$ 166.67) monthly you can have approximately R$ 1 million (US$ 340,000) with 48-49 years old. Since in the simulation I have considered inflation effects the same money power of 1 million today will be after that long period.

Ayurvedic Financial Freedom: Insights From My Wealth Journey

In the following chapters I will present my family real personal data, which involved the achievement of an amount of money of R$ 1 million in less than the 28-29 years indicated in the last plan presented, since we did and increasing amount savings during our financial freedom journey. In addition, next I will discuss a little about other insights besides compound interesting in order to encourage you to follow a similar journey. If you want to share with me your insights from your financial freedom journey please e-mail me (diego_tresinari@yahoo.com.br). It would be a pleasure to receive an email from you.

Chapter 7

INSIGHTS FROM MY FINANCIAL FREEDOM JOURNEY: INVEST AIMING FINANCIAL FREEDOM

"Ce soir je prend le large. Sans savoir ou je vais. Je suivrais les étoile. Ce soir je prend le large. Je vis ma destine. Mon chemin c'est ma liberté".

(Text in French)

"Tonight I'm sailing away. Without knowing where I'll go. I'll just follow the star. Tonight I'm sailing away. I'm living my destiny. My road is my freedom."

Tal Benyerzi (French Singer)

Of course the impact as described in the chapter before of compound interest is enormous in any financial freedom journey since with continuous compounding, any interest earned immediately begins earning interest on itself. On the other hand, my own experience demonstrated that the insight "Invest aiming financial freedom" has similar relevance as well the others presented further.

Financial freedom is the status of having enough income to pay one's living expenses for the rest of one's life without having to be employed or dependent on others. In this book I avoided the terminology mostly common used "financial independence" since, as country history shows, to become independent is different from to become free. And, how can I start from the beginning of my financial freedom journey investing money thinking about financial freedom, since the target point is so far away? Yes, this is one of the best paradoxes that you can find in finances. If you invest in a debt instrument with promise to pay back the money with a fixed interest like Bonds, for instance, the larger is the time horizon that you have to leave your money in this investment the higher will be the fixed interest that you can get. So the idea of having a very organized financial plan that allows you to keep an amount of money "blocked" during a fixed time horizon is a very good strategy to reduce the time for achieving financial freedom point (in Spain and Argentine, for instance, the name of this kind of investment is "Depósito a Plazo Fijo", fixed-term deposit). In reality not all debt instrument blocks money, some you can sell before the time horizon defined and sometimes with valorization that can boost even more your investment return. As this strategy is similar to the one that well trained investors do in the Stock market using Fundamental and/or Chart analyses, I will not get into this subject in this book. On the other hand, if you want to learn it, you can contact me (diego_tresinari@yahoo.com.br) and we can arrange a way to have a meeting. As I continue travelling around the word, now for leisure and not more for scientific working purposes since I quit my formal job in 2018, maybe I can pass near you and we can have a personal meeting.

In Figure 6 and Table 2 it is presented the personal real data of my financial freedom journey until the end of 2018. It is also indicated the impact in investment return gained by the use of the strategy "Invest aiming financial freedom". When compared to the simulated strategy previously, that consider an fixed saving amount monthly, as we can see in Figure 6, we can conclude that the investment return and the compounding/saving amount ratio were similar over the period considered (11 years). Indeed, a similar real investment return around 5-6 % per year was obtained, considering an inflation rate of 5 % and an approximate interest rate of 9-10 % per year. Obviously to use this strategy you have first to keep a fixed amount of your savings in an investment that you can withdraw the money anytime that you want. After the construction of this emergency fund, that I commonly recommend to keep at least an amount equivalent of 6 to 12 times your expenses, you are safe to use my insight.

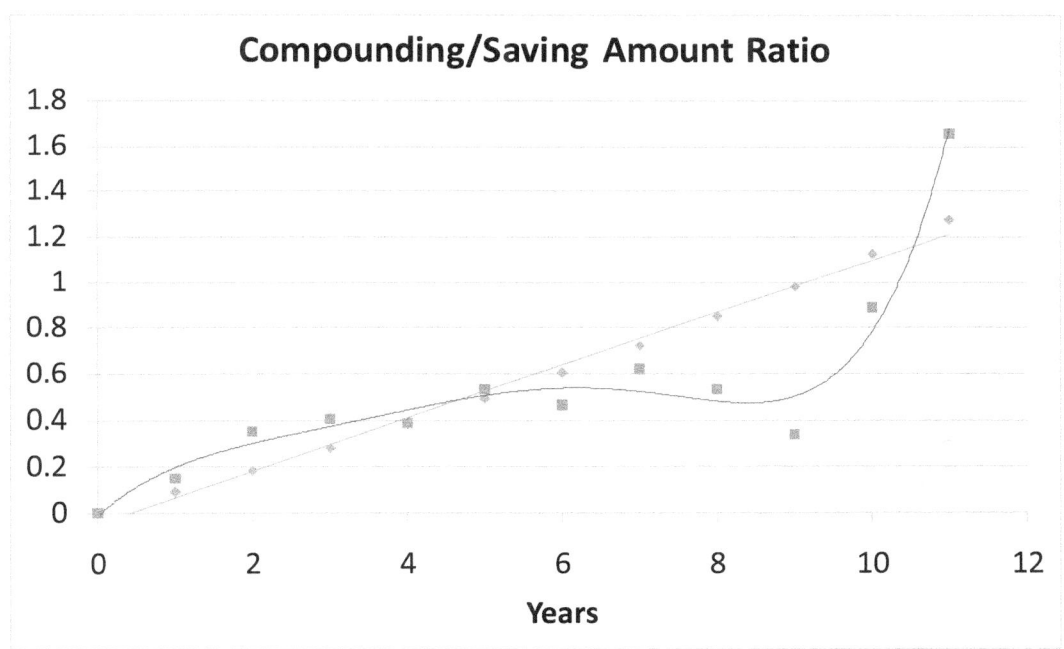

Figure 6. Compounding/saving amount ratio effect over time (plotted in ■ using my real personal data - Compounding is related to Compound Interest + Asset Valorization Amount and in ◊ using simulated data - Compounding is related to only Compound Interest Amount).

Table 2. Equity compounding/saving amount ratio evaluation effect over time using personal real data.

Year	Saving Amount (Monthly)	Saving Amount	Equity	Compound Interest + Asset Valorization Amount	Compound Interest + Asset Valorization/ Saving Amount Ratio
1 (2008)	R$ 833.33	R$ 10,000.00	R$ 10,000.00	R$ 1,500.00	0.150
2 (2009)	R$ 2,400.00	R$ 28,800.00	R$ 40,300.00	R$ 10,075.00	0.350
3 (2010)	R$ 2,500.00	R$ 30,000.00	R$ 80,375.00	R$ 12,056.25	0.402
4 (2011)	R$ 4,928.72	R$ 59,144.69	R$ 151,575.94	R$ 22,736.39	0.384
5 (2012)	R$ 5,221.69	R$ 62,660.26	R$ 236,972.59	R$ 33,176.16	0.529
6 (2013)	R$ 13,101.11	R$ 157,213.36	R$ 427,362.11	R$ 72,651.56	0.462
7 (2014)	R$ 6,174.25	R$ 74,090.99	R$ 574,104.66	R$ 45,928.37	0.620
8 (2015)	R$ 12,033.58	R$ 144,403.00	R$ 764,436.04	R$ 76,443.60	0.529
9 (2016)	R$ 21,128.11	R$ 253,537.36	R$ 1,094,417.00	R$ 85,807.13	0.338
10 (2017)	R$ 6,269.53	R$ 75,234.30	R$ 1,255,458.43	R$ 66,648.97	0.886
11 (2018)	R$ 4,096.10	R$ 49,153.20	R$ 1,371,260.60	R$ 81,289.52	1.654

Differently from the simulation done previously, what you can see here, is that instead of only having passive income from investments, as we can get when investing in Bonds, for example, my wife and I saw our Equity not linear increase by the combination of Compound Interest plus estimated Asset Valorization (Figure 6). In 2009, for example, we got our first mortgage loan to buy a 2-bedroom Apartment that we finished to pay it in 2013 and lived until the beginning of 2018. Additionally, we got another two mortgage loans to buy two lands for construction rental Real Estate properties, which we bought in 2011 and 2013, and finished paying them in 2013 and 2015, respectively. Since the mortgage loans that we got were only for a very short period of time, 2 to 4 years, it didn't impact negatively in our financial freedom path as this strategy was used as financial leverage. Leverage is an investment strategy of using borrowed money - specifically, the use of financial instruments or borrowed capital - to increase the potential return of an investment and/or to finance assets.

So, until 2015 I used Financial Leverage and from that to now I have changed my strategy to "intelligent" use of bonds and stocks (considering timing strategies; i.e. buying and selling them in opportune periods) as this last strategy demonstrated to be more appropriate to one that invests aiming financial freedom. As you can see in Figure 6, the Compound

Interest + Asset Valorization/Saving Amount Ratio (plotted in ■) over time was very oscillatory and the return obtained was not so different from that one that could be obtained with Brazilian debt instruments with a fixed interest.

Chapter 8

INSIGHTS FROM MY FINANCIAL FREEDOM JOURNEY: DEFINE YOUR LIFE STYLE

"Think a lot about life style if you want to live your financial life with any style."

Diego Tresinari

Again I started another chapter with my own quote. "Think a lot about life style if you want to live your life with any style." can sound a little bit childish. Otherwise, from my perspective I would like to emphasize the necessity of self responsibility for financial freedom candidates.

Independently were you live, in a poor or rich country, it would be very difficult to find in your neighbourhood a financial freedom person or in your family. So it is obviously that you cannot copy their habits and behaviours. Most of the people in the word are living a very automatic life. They are living in a similar way of an ant. On the other hand, as a human being you have the choice to live your life with your own life style. Unfortunately, excluding lottery winners or someone that bought Bitcoins in its beginnings, I do not know any feasible and reproducible way to easily get financial freedom fast.

Thus, as a first exercise, think about the way that you had being living until today. Have you done the same things that your parents, friends and colleagues from work have done: did you get a University degree, got marriage, bought a car and a house, had kids, and so on? If your answer was yes, yes and yes and you are not financially free probably you were just following the life like others without thinking. As I have mentioned before, I am not a totally alternative person. I did the same things as my peers, but in a different way. And that small difference made all difference for my personal finances.

My wife and I met in University back in 2003. We both started in the same year at the Chemical Engineering course at the best University of

Brazil, the University of São Paulo (USP). Different from other countries, the best universities in Brazil are free of charge but it is very difficult to get in as you have to go though several tests and get good grades. The University that we got in was away from our parents' house, so we shared Apartments with friends. If back in 2003 we decided, or had the only option, to get a loan to pay our University degree and live near our parents, as some of our old friends from high school did, our life would probably be very different. Probably we wouldn't be talking about financial freedom and our early retirement would be just a dream.

During University, after we have enjoyed intensively the parties and the University environment and friends, without the presence of our parents, we started thinking about how to get our own money, as until 2005, all of our own expenses were being paid buy our parents. Thus, my wife and I (that time she was only my friend) started doing research in a laboratory of the University to get a fellowship of R$ 300. That time my father was giving me R$ 600, monthly, for my own total expenses. As my father would continue paying this amount until I get my University degree (end of 2007), I started saving money to develop my first financial plan, which at that time, would involve my friend Juliana that would become my girlfriend and wife sequentially.

Our financial plan involved improving our language skills of Spanish and English using the minimal amount of money as possible. Again, thinking outside the box, and in a very different way that our friends were doing: paying very expensive language schools and institutional internships. After we started dating, we decided to live together to spend less money in rent. Additionally, we started working in extra jobs to increase our income.

So, during 2006-2008, with our extra earned money, we travelled together to Chile, Argentine, Uruguay, Ireland, Northern Ireland, United Kingdom and France. As a result, we improved our language skills as planned, but also we had improved our professional skills as in Chile and Ireland we worked as researchers in their University laboratories. The experience was very important and decisive to the master and Ph.D. fellowship selections.

Then, in March of 2008 we finished our first financial plan successfully and started from zero (without any money saved). On the other hand, we had two approved master fellowships in a different city from where we went to University and also we had a very good felling of partnership and commitment constructed that still shapes our loving relationship.

Below (Figure 7 and Table 3) you will find our cash flow data staring from 2008.

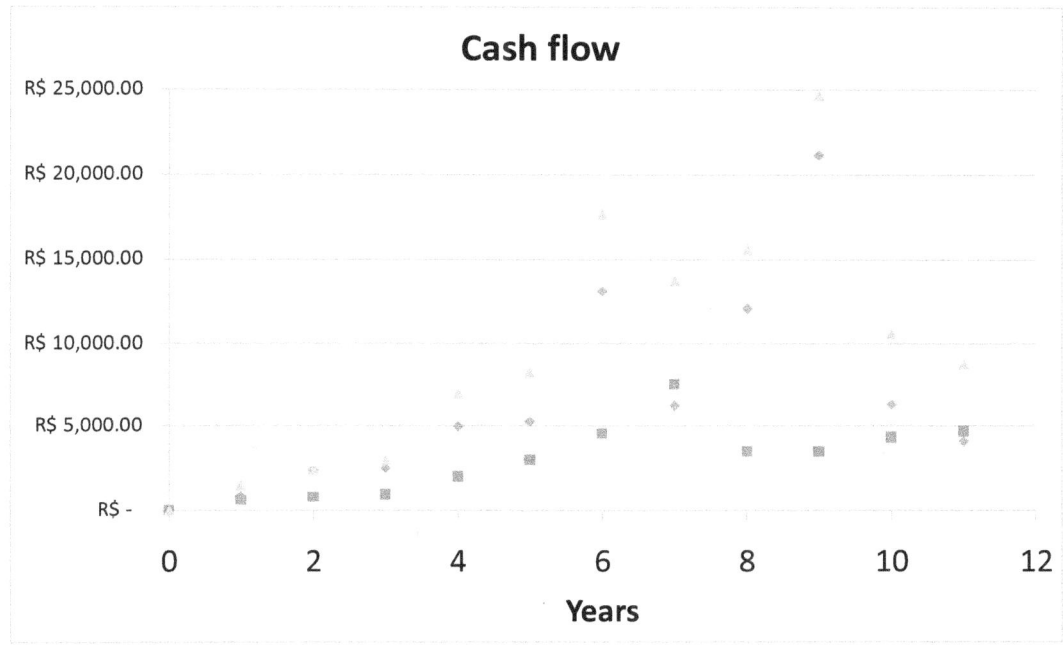

Figure 7. Cash flow effect over time using personal real data (plotted in ▲: Salary Income (Monthly); ◊: Saving Amount (Monthly); ■: General Expenses (Monthly).

Table 3. Percentage of income from salary saved evaluation effect over time using personal real data.

Year	Salary Income (Monthly)	Annual Salary Income	General Expenses (Monthly)	Annual General Expenses	Percentage of income from Salary saved
1 (2008)	R$ 1,455.00	R$ 17,460.00	R$ 600.00	R$ 7,200.00	57.27
2 (2009)	R$ 2,400.00	R$ 28,800.00	R$ 750.00	R$ 9,000.00	100
3 (2010)	R$ 3,000.00	R$ 36,000.00	R$ 916.67	R$ 11,000.00	83.33
4 (2011)	R$ 6,928.72	R$ 83,144.69	R$ 2,000.00	R$ 24,000.00	71.13
5 (2012)	R$ 8,221.69	R$ 98,660.26	R$ 3,000.00	R$ 36,000.00	63.51
6 (2013)	R$ 17,601.11	R$ 211,213.36	R$ 4,500.00	R$ 54,000.00	74.43
7 (2014)	R$ 13,674.25	R$ 164,090.99	R$ 7,500.00	R$ 90,000.00	45.15
8 (2015)	R$ 15,533.58	R$ 186,403.00	R$ 3,500.00	R$ 42,000.00	77.47
9 (2016)	R$ 24,628.11	R$ 295,537.36	R$ 3,500.00	R$ 42,000.00	85.79
10 (2017)	R$ 10,569.53	R$ 126,834.30	R$ 4,300.00	R$ 51,600.00	59.32
11 (2018)	R$ 8,756.10	R$ 105,073.20	R$ 4,660.00	R$ 55,920.00	46.78

It can be seem, that from the beginning (2008) until Year 9 (2016) of our financial freedom plan, our Salary (plotted in ▲ in Figure 7) has increased exponentially as our Savings (plotted in ◊ in Figure 7), meanwhile our Expenses increased in a linear way until Year 7 (2014).

Our first kid was born in 2011 (Year 4), so the linear increase of our Expenses was a very naturally behavior.

In the beginning, we spent most of the time at the University that we were working and we didn't have much time to spend our salary. In addition, we used to eat at the University restaurant as the price was very cheap. Thus, we restricted a lot our expenses; meanwhile we started finding ways to increase our income. The direct result of it can be seen by the parameter "Percentage of income from Salary saved" from Table 3. Until Year 7 (2014) it varied from 57-100 %. The number of 100% obtained in 2009 was due to the use of financial leverage applied in the Apartment that we bought, when we rented the spare bedroom. So, we used our salary to pay as much as we could the mortgage, reducing the amount of paid interests, and paid our expenses using the earned money from the rent. Therefore, since we started our financial freedom path we could see the miracle effect of the using your investment to generate ourselves income. This kind of income is commonly referred as passive income as you "in theory" do not have to be active, like working in a common job, to generate it. Here I preferred only emphasized the terminology "Salary income" as there are several other ways to generate income, as rent from Real Estate Properties and/or indirectly with the valorization of an asset. Table 4 demonstrates the effect of "Compound Interest + Asset Valorization Amount" over the years and its influence together with the saved amount in the achievement of the financial freedom point. To estimated the Financial Freedom parameter, it was considerate the inclusion of inflation impact, and it was estimated based on the previous years that 40 % of our earnings from investments could be left to keep money value.

Table 4. Financial freedom point evaluation effect over time using personal real data.

Year	Saving Amount (Monthly)	General Expenses (Monthly)	Compound Interest + Asset Valorization Amount (Monthly)	Profitability (%)	Financial Freedom Point
1 (2008)	R$ 833.33	R$ 600.00	R$ 125.00	15	0.125
2 (2009)	R$ 2,400.00	R$ 750.00	R$ 839.58	25	0.672
3 (2010)	R$ 2,500.00	R$ 916.67	R$ 1,004.69	15	0.658
4 (2011)	R$ 4,928.72	R$ 2,000.00	R$ 1,894.70	15	0.568

5 (2012)	R$ 5,221.69	R$ 3,000.00	R$ 2,764.68	14	0.553
6 (2013)	R$ 13,101.11	R$ 4,500.00	R$ 6,054.30	17	0.807
7 (2014)	R$ 6,174.25	R$ 7,500.00	R$ 3,827.36	8	0.306
8 (2015)	R$ 12,033.58	R$ 3,500.00	R$ 6,370.30	10	1.092
9 (2016)	R$ 21,128.11	R$ 3,500.00	R$ 7,150.59	8	1.226
10 (2017)	R$ 6,269.53	R$ 4,300.00	R$ 5,554.08	5	0.775
11 (2018)	R$ 4,096.10	R$ 4,660.00	R$ 6,774.13	6	0.872

It can be seem, that after Year 6 (2013) the profitability originated from our investments, measured here by the combined effect of Compound Interest + Asset Valorization, was reduced to the range of 5 to 10 % per year. This was mostly due to the effect of Economic Crisis in Brazil that stopped the continuous valorization of our Real Estate Properties. As we were at that time with most of our Equity concentrated in the Apartment that we lived and two lands, we suffered the impact of this Economic Crisis in our financial freedom plan.

Then, in 2014 (Year 7) our family returned from Switzerland. At that time we were a family of 4, my 3 year old son, my pregnant wife and me. I started studying about investment portfolio diversification, stock market, chart analysis, macroeconomics, engineering economics and so on. In parallel, my wife and I started thinking about our life style. If you take a look at the Financial Freedom Point parameter in Table 4 you can see that in the year that we were living in Switzerland (2014) this parameter reduced from 0.80724 to 0.306189. As the Financial Freedom is achieved when this parameter is 1 or higher, we understood that our expenses played a key factor that we were underestimating.

Therefore, after defining our life style in an attentive way, we reduced our monthly expenses to R$ 3,500.00 (which represented a reduction of 22.22%). This value was kept constant during Year 8 (2015) and Year 9 (2016). It can be thought in a first glimpse that we had restricted a lot our expenses. But I ensure you that we didn't change anything that could cause us a bad felling, as I already told you in Chapter 4. On the opposite, with that reduction from R$ 4,500.00 to R$ 3,500.00 we increased a lot our felling of freedom and self responsibility.

Chapter 9

INSIGHTS FROM MY FINANCIAL FREEDOM JOURNEY: DEFINE A SAFE WITHDRAWAL RATE

"They say: Think twice before you jump. I say: Jump first and then think as much as you want!"

Osho (Indian Spiritual Teacher)

After "using compound interest in your favour", "investing aiming financial freedom" and "defining your life style", finally, we get to the final step of our journey "Spending the safe earned interest Step". If you achieve that step, and I hope that you will sooner than you expect, this is the moment that you can quit your job and start only living from the earning interests from your money.

I started writing this book in October 2017 and today it is March of 2020, more than 2 years have passed, and some good surprises had occurred. The most relevant was the birth of my third kid, a baby girl, in 2018, which again was responsible for a increase of my Kapha nature. Hence, my wife and I decided to take a sabbatical period to take care of our new baby and family. Today probably I do not have anymore that 10 % Kapha mentioned before. Meanwhile we were in this sabbatical period, we decided to stop working forever. As it can be seen in Table 4, at that time, we had not achieved the financial freedom point, but since I was performing very well in the stock and bond markets we could increase the income by getting a higher profitability. Therefore, this last chapter has a completely different approach. The title for example is "Define a safe withdrawal rate". The word safe is complete opposite as the key meaning of the quote that I selected to start this chapter. Having this paradoxical start, I will talk about the last years of my financial freedom journey.

We mathematically achieved the financial freedom point (1.09, Table 4) at Year 8 (2015) by reducing our expenses. At the subsequently year, the financial freedom point increased to 1.23 as we decided to accept the invitation of going to Spain to a postdoctoral period. It was possible to increase our savings as the living costs in Spain are much lower than in Switzerland and are similar to Brazil. In this way, Year 9 (2016) was the year that we had the highest Saving Amount (R$ 21,128.11 Monthly) (Figure 7, Table 4). But at that time, we have realized that travelling with the kids, as they were getting older, was getting more complicated. They struggled to adapt in a new country and missed a lot their friends and family from Brazil. So, after arriving in Brazil at 2016, we decided to reduce our income from salary accepting lower pay checks in order to slow down our agitated life. We decided to spend only 2 to 3 months abroad when necessary in order to respect the will of the kids of belonging, not taking them way for too long from their friends and community in Brazil, but at the same time indulging our desire to explore and travel. As we are very committed to freedom, my wife and I, after living in different cultures and studying about education, decided to unschool/worldschool our kids. We believed that kids (as well as adults) should be free in order to learn what is necessary or important to their life, and that the school system usually kills the joy and will for learning. Although it was a big decision, it was a relatively easy one. The kids really enjoy learning out of school and it is amazing how fast and deep they learn with love. I must say it also represented a big saving of money for us, in spite of not being the goal of our decision, as good schools that use more respectful pedagogies in Brazil are private and very expensive. Consequently, the following years (Years 10 and 11, 2017 and 2018, respectively), after we arrived at the financial freedom point, the parameter reduced to lower than 1 (0.77 and 0.87), indicating that we had technically lost our financial freedom condition.

We started the year 2019 (Year 12) with the financial controversy decision to take a sabbatical period and move from our own Apartment to a rented bigger house. In contrast, having the Osho's quote and a similar phrase of a close friend in mind, I tried to jump into an experiment of transforming the sabbatical period of 1 year in the first year of our early retirement (we were 33 years old). Seeing that I was getting sequentially gains doing trading with bonds and stocks since 2015, I decided to increase the amount of money invested in it and surprisingly it worked. I have obtained a similar performance of the last 4 years, but as I increased the amount of money in this strategy, the amount of earnings increased together. It resulted in the highest financial freedom point value achieved until now (1.41), despite of the biggest monthly expense of R$ 10.000. The increase in the monthly expense was also higher as it was the first time we spent 2 months abroad with our own money. Usually, we stayed abroad working having all our expenses paid by our contractor. I must say it is the only part of my job that I miss. But this year we were at our sabbatical period and it was the first time we paid everything, from plane tickets to housing, ourselves. We spent two months in Spain living in a city with a large uschooling/worldschooling community, with people from all over the world.

So, for the following years, our financial freedom will be guaranteed if I keep the same investing method applied in 2019 and if it works. It sounds unsafe, isn't it? But for early retirees with a personality like ours, we have found the best way to spend our lives. As the amount of money gained in 2019 was far than enough to pay the expenses of the entire year of 2019 we kept the extra amount to increase our assets. Then, we have the following 16 months expenses guaranteed, excluding the compounding effect of the money, which can guarantee the payment of some additional few months. During the initial months of 2020 I guaranteed with my financial trading gains another additional 7 months of paid expenses, following our chosen consciously daily life style.

Most of the comments from different authors about safe withdrawal rate for early retirees are very technical and commonly are not from people that are living it. Around 2016, I started wondering about it and I was not very happy with the idea of having a very strict budget every month. My Vata energy was felling uncomfortable about this claustrophobic situation. If you do not have much Vata energy in yourself, probably you cannot understand me. But if you have it, you will fell some empathy. Thus, I finalize this book with a very unfamiliar chapter.

Chapter 10

ANTI-GUIDELINES FOR PERFORMING AN AYURVEDIC FINANCIAL FREEDOM JOURNEY

"Freedom is only an opportunity for you. It is not in itself the goal. It simply gives you the whole opportunity to do whatever you want to do. Now you are free and you are feeling sad, because you have not used this opportunity yet. Meditation will do, music will do, sculpture will do, dancing will do, love will do. But do something with your freedom. Just don't sit with your freedom, otherwise you will become sad."

Osho (Indian Spiritual Teacher)

This last chapter I have written thinking about my dear wife, who I also dedicate this book. This is my first non scientific book and I know that it is not as perfect as I would like it to be. Then, she besides my partner during my financial freedom journey is also the editor of this book.

In different periods both of us have passed for the sadness that Osho describes in the quote of this chapter. After the blissfully experiencing of achieving financial freedom point we both had experiencing the felling of a very different sadness. I would name it emptiness. It is a kind of lack of energy (most specifically Pitta-type energy if you use Ayurvedic vision), as we do not need to be so tense and hungry to get money anymore. In addition, as our desires for getting luxurious things stopped very earlier, due to our understanding that some of these desires came from society combined with some lack of inner strength, I think that this sad period lasted. Then, from my heart I really desire that you can have such a sad/empty felling after some months of achieving your financial freedom point. On the other hand, I expect that you pass through this experience and achieve the Financial Freedom Wealth. You can name it differently, but the idea is that you get to a point where money is not an issue to you.

It can look like that some beggar, poor or religious people got the same point, but it is not the same. On contrary, I have found some rich people saying that they are not afraid of losing their money and I also tell you that they also didn't get to the point that I am talking. Therefore, I invite you to take the financial freedom journey and enjoy the freedom regardless of this sadness feeling that will settle in the end.

My guidelines for performing a financial freedom journey towards Ayurvedic Financial Freedom is:

1) do not follow any guidelines from anyone, including myself;

2) have enough courage for doubting your mind;

3) do not focus much in the money, focus in the enjoyment of the financial journey;

4) get people involved in it, travelling by yourself can be lonely;

5) do not be very strict about your finances, mathematics is only a tool and should not become the master;

6) it is a pity not having the experiencing of getting financial freedom in life, so start it right now independently of your age;

7) you are not your carrier and you are not your function (mother, father, son, husband, etc.);

8) you can learn from life much more than from books;

9) all that you are felling right now are the result from what you have being fed. Feed yourself with good food for all your senses (sight, hearing, smell, taste and touch) (this is the basic principle of Ayurveda);

10) freedom is the most import thing in life;

11) accept yourself as you are, but remember that you can find some partners to perform a perfect plan;

12) "don't ask the barber whether you need a haircut" (Warren Buffett's quote - American business magnate, investor, and philanthropist, one of the richest investors in the world).

Diego Tresinari

March 2020

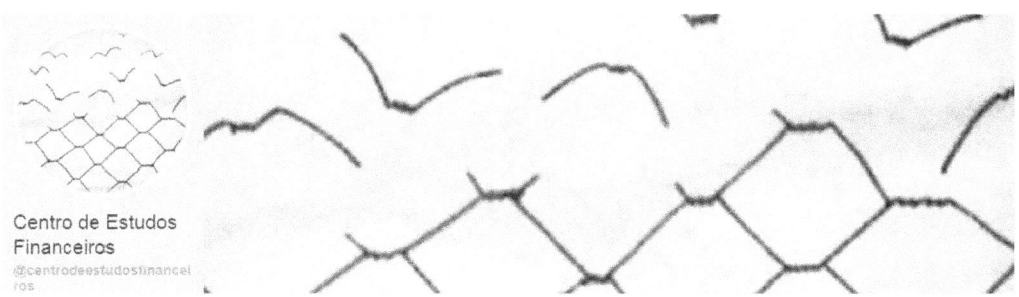

CENTER FOR FINANCIAL STUDIES (FINANCIAL CONSULTING, BRAZIL)

"We help you to learn how invest money through mentoring programs (In English, Spanish or Portuguese)"

There are on-line mentoring programs to learn to Invents from Real State, Bonds, Stocks, Cryptocurrencies (Bitcoin), and so on, using different methods (Fundamental and Chart/Technical Analysis) (The programs are suitable for Financial Markets Worldwide).

Diego Tresnari, Ph.D.
Scientific Researcher (Engineering Economics/Food Science and Technology)
Campinas-SP, Brazil
E-mail: diego_tresnari@yahoo.com.br
WhatsApp: +55.19.99805.0484

CENTER FOR AYURVEDIC STUDIES (FOOD SCIENCE AND AYURVEDA, BRAZIL)

"We help you to balance your life through mentoring programs following Ayurveda Teachings (In English, Spanish or Portuguese)"

There are on-line mentoring programs to balance your health and lifestyle and promote self-knowledge. Such a multidimensional Ayurvedic life plan consists of guidelines regarding diet, nutritional supplements, healing herbs, yoga, meditation, relaxation and stress management techniques, gentle cleansing and detoxification, massage, special daily and seasonal routines, Ayurveda can help to assist in body-mind issues and diseases.

Diego Tresinari, Ph.D.
Scientific Researcher (Engineering Economics/Food Science and Technology)
Campinas-SP, Brazil
E-mail: diego_tresinari@yahoo.com.br
WhatsApp: +55.19.99805.0484

OTHER BOOKS: LIBERDADE FINANCEIRA AYURVÉDICA: INSIGHTS DE MINHA JORNADA (PORTUGUESE EDITION)

Liberdade Financeira Ayurvédica, originalmente publicado em inglês em março de 2020 com o título Ayurvedic Financial Freedom, é um livro sobre como você pode usar o melhor de si mesmo para se tornar financeiramente independente. Na direção oposta da maioria dos renomados livros e gurus do enriquecimento, este livro se concentra em saber que devemos assumir o controle de nossa vida financeira e buscar liberdade e paz interior. A etapa de autoconhecimento é conduzida usando os tradicionais sistemas orientais Ayurveda e Mindfulness para expor as ilusões da mente e trazer nosso corpo-mente de volta ao equilíbrio. O conhecimento dos 3 biotipos do Ayurveda, Vata, Pitta e Kapha, é usado para compreender nossa própria personalidade, a fim de expor nossas forças e fraquezas em relação à questões financeiras. O primeiro passo da jornada é abraçar nossa personalidade e usar o melhor dela para definir um plano de liberdade financeira. Estar ciente de nossas emoções, impulsos e necessidades no momento presente nos manterá com as rédeas na mão. Além disso, este livro o convida a descobrir como pode ser emocionante e surpreendente o caminho até chegar à liberdade financeira. Como pano de fundo, é utilizada minha própria jornada e experiência de liberdade financeira, o que resultou em muitos exemplos práticos e histórias engraçadas. Também são expostos alguns conceitos que pesquisei sobre engenharia econômica durante meu doutorado e estudos de pós-doutoramento.

(https://www.amazon.com.br/Liberdade-Financeira-Ayurv%C3%A9dica-Insights-Jornada-ebook/dp/B08LMZSWZT)

OTHER BOOKS: AÇÕES COM LUCIDEZ: A SAGA DE UM INVESTIDOR INICIANTE NA BOLSA DE VALORES (PORTUGUESE EDITION)

O livro "Ações com Lucidez" apresenta o detalhamento da saga de um Investidor iniciante na renda fixa (Tesouro Direto) e na renda variável (Ações da Bolsa de Valores e Fundos de Investimentos Imobiliários, FIIs). Em linguagem simples e acessível este livro foi formulado através da compilação de documentos publicados na página do facebook do Centro de Estudos Financeiros (www.facebook.com.br/centrodeestudosfinanceiros) durante o ano de 2019, utilizando dados reais de um cliente que eu vinha prestando sessões de mentoria financeira desde 2017. O referido cliente se enquadra em um perfil que possivelmente deva ser similar ao da grande maioria dos Brasileiros: estava preocupado com a fase de sua aposentadoria, reforma da previdência social, etc.; sabia algo sobre Imóveis e nada sobre investimentos no mercado financeiro. (https://www.amazon.com.br/dp/B08C8ZZFNC/ref=cm_sw_r_wa_awdo_t1_wJNaFbKYRG0KM)

OTHER BOOKS: – INVESTIDOR-TRADER LÚCIDO: ACABANDO COM A POLARIZAÇÃO NO MUNDO DOS INVESTIMENTOS (PORTUGUESE EDITION)

O livro "Investidor-Trader Lúcido: Acabando com a Polarização no Mundo dos Investimentos" apresenta o detalhamento da minha dinâmica durante a tomada decisão na renda variável (Ações da Bolsa de Valores, Fundos de Investimentos Imobiliários, Criptomoedas e Mini-contratos Futuros) usando uma visão holística e nada usual, que utiliza tanto ferramentas que os Investidores usam: Análise Fundamentalista, assim como as que os Traders comumente fazem uso: Análise Gráfica. Em linguagem simples e acessível este livro foi formulado através da compilação de 7 documentos publicados mês a mês (de junho a dezembro) na página do facebook do Centro de Estudos Financeiros durante o ano de 2020, utilizando dados reais de meus investimentos/operações pessoais e/ou de mentorados que dou mentoria financeira. Após 3 operações com mini-contratos de dólar e 4 investimentos/operações com ações utilizando a "Metodologia Zen" que faz uso da Análise Gráfica usando Candles semanais, o que possibilita acompanhar o mercado somente 1 h por semana às sextas-feiras durante o período da tarde, foi-se obtido uma rentabilidade no período (7 meses) de 37,24 %, o que representa uma rentabilidade anualizada de 63,84 % (se somente considerarmos os ganhos com ações, sem considerar os ganhos com mercado futuro obteve-se uma rentabilidade de 43,15 % ao ano; próximo da média obtida ano a ano desde 2013)(https://www.amazon.com.br/dp/B08RCGYPV7?ref_=cm_sw_r_kb_dp_xyD7Fb1FW2ZBQ&tag=kp014-20&linkCode=kpe).

BOOK SERIES (AMAZON) – INVESTIMENTOS COM LUCIDEZ (PORTUGUESE EDITION)

Todos os livros acima fazem parta da série de livros: Investimentos com Lucidez. Ainda serão lançados brevemente os livros: Imóveis com Lucidez e Renda Fixa com Lucidez que farão parte desta série, bem como possivelmente outros relacionados à temática finanças e investimentos, assim que para acompanhar o lançamento dos próximos livros acesse o link: https://www.amazon.com/-/pt/gp/product/B08NGPLYNM?ref_=dbs_dp_rwt_sb_tkin&binding=kindle_edition.

A série Investimentos com Lucidez é uma série que contém livros que abordam tanto os temas finanças pessoais e investimentos [Renda Fixa, Tesouro Direto, Ações, Dólar, Fundos Imobiliários, Imóveis, Investimentos Responsáveis (ESG): investimentos sustentáveis e socialmente responsáveis, Criptomoedas, etc.] quanto autoconhecimento e surge de um projeto pessoal que brotou na reta final de minha jornada de liberdade/independência financeira. Iniciado em 2008 a minha jornada financeira foi se entrelaçando durante os anos com a minha jornada de autoconhecimento e culminou no primeiro livro da série: Ayurvedic

Financial Freedom: Insights From My Wealth Journey (2020), que posteriormente foi traduzido para o Português recebendo o título: Liberdade Financeira Ayurvédica: Insights de Minha Jornada. Este é um livro sobre como você pode usar o melhor de si mesmo para se tornar financeiramente independente. Na direção oposta da maioria dos renomados livros e gurus do enriquecimento, este livro se concentra em saber que devemos assumir o controle de nossa vida financeira e buscar liberdade e paz interior. A etapa de autoconhecimento é conduzida usando os tradicionais sistemas orientais Ayurveda e Mindfulness para expor as ilusões da mente e trazer nosso corpo-mente de volta ao equilíbrio. O conhecimento dos 3 biotipos do Ayurveda, Vata, Pitta e Kapha, é usado para compreender nossa própria personalidade, a fim de expor nossas forças e fraquezas em relação à questões financeiras. Assim que o primeiro passo da jornada é abraçar nossa personalidade e usar o melhor dela para definir um plano de liberdade financeira, estando ciente de nossas emoções, impulsos e necessidades no momento presente para nos manter com as rédeas na mão.

www.ingramcontent.com/pod-product-compliance
Lightning Source LLC
Chambersburg PA
CBHW081437220526
45466CB00008B/2419